Silhouettes of the

GREAT WESTERN

R. J. BLENKINSOP

© 1976 Oxford Publishing Co.

Published by
Oxford Publishing Co.
8 The Roundway
Risinghurst, Oxford, England.

SBN 902888 63 3

Printed by B. H. Blackwell (Printing) Ltd
in the City of Oxford

Photo reproduction and offset plates
by Oxford Litho Plates Ltd.

PREFACE

When I started Railway photography in 1948 it never occurred to me that the steam engine would ever be replaced by a better means of motive power.

Like many other enthusiasts I have witnessed and recorded the height of post-war engine work and also the decline which started in the early 1960s and was wound up with the last steam-hauled passenger train in August 1968.

So far as the Western Region was concerned it seemed to me that the end of steam came after the "King" Class engines were all withdrawn before the beginning of 1963. They had been the main express passenger engine on the Paddington-Wolverhampton line nearby where I live, so obviously when they were replaced by the "Western" Class diesel-hydraulics the bottom fell out of my railway photographic operation.

In fact there was still plenty of interest to see in the last years of British Steam but the engines became less cared for and this state of neglect did not inspire me to spend many hours by the railway with the chance of one or two clean engines in a day's photography.

I therefore decided that this book would be the fourth and last in the present series as I could end conveniently with the demise of the "Kings". In 1963 No. 6018 **King Henry VI** was operational on at least two special trains in the early part of the year, but it was not until that wonderful day in October 1971 that I saw No. 6000 **King George V** in action again.

In 1960 I purchased a new Leica M.2 with a 50 mm f.2 Summicron lens. This book is a tribute to the designers and manufacturers of this camera, Ernst Leitz G.m.b.H. of Wetzlar, Germany, who of course invented the 35 mm camera. Looking back at the decision to buy a good camera was difficult at the time in financial terms, but I realise that for once I made a correct choice.

The camera fulfilled every requirement I could make on it for a 35 mm instrument and it has never once let me down or been repaired. Today it still operates with a quality and precision where the limiting factor is my own capability.

All the photographs in this album except three were taken with the Leica and the majority on Ilford FP.3 film developed in Promicrol.

As in the three previous albums all the pictures are in date order and are selected to provide a feast of happy memories for those of us who were and are influenced by the magic spell of the steam railway locomotive.

I have included a number of photographs taken at Old Oak Common locomotive depot and also at Paddington station. Both these places have an atmosphere of their own which is quite unique.

"Old Oak" on a Sunday morning with its enormous engine house containing four turntables, provided a feast of sleeping engines having a rest day due to the limited Sunday services. All this was brought back to me a few weeks ago when I called to check on some information and found the smell of diesel oil supreme. The scene has completely changed due to the engine house being demolished and only the bare concrete floor remaining.

Paddington was never an easy place for photography. The best time was in the late afternoon when the sun's rays fell on the front of the engines lined up at the platforms awaiting departure during the evening rush.

A variety of changes took place in the period under review and not only can they be seen in the photographs, but many of the locations have also altered dramatically.

I do hope you have enjoyed the four volumes in this series which show some of the work of a railway photographer, in chronological order, covering a period of exactly 11 years beginning in October 1951.

1   I am starting the book with one of the fastest trains on the Western Region. The 13.15 Paddington-Bristol was allowed two hours for the 118¼ miles, including a stop at Bath.

No. 6015 **King Richard III** was travelling over 70 m.p.h. when this photograph was taken at the west end of Sonning Cutting, near Reading.

19 April 1960

2 Both engines seem to be taking water at the same time quite satisfactorily in this scene at Goring troughs. With a load of 14 bogies No. 5051 **Earl Bathurst** has No. 5980 **Dingley Hall** as pilot with an afternoon express from Paddington to Bristol.

19 April 1960

3 In making my way westwards towards Didcot a country road crosses the main line adjacent to Moreton yard some 1½ miles east of Didcot station.

In the low evening sun No. 7035 **Ogmore Castle** is in charge of the "Cheltenham Spa Express" which had its first stop at Kemble. The double chimney on the "Castles" never looked right although I must have photographed it from every conceivable angle.

19 April 1960

4

2-8-0 No. 4705 is seen leaving Didcot for Swindon with a stopping train, having departed from Reading at 17.16. The engine looks fairly clean so was probably on a return "running in" turn from Swindon.

The bedraggled engine on the left of the picture is No. 4078 **Pembroke Castle** waiting at the signals with an up freight.

19 April 1960

5

While the express passenger train had all the glory shed on it — usually because it was fast and clean — I often preferred the fascination of the goods train rattling past with its variety of wagons and load.

In this scene No. 4946 **Moseley Hall** passes Croes Newydd shed with an up freight carrying class "K" headlamps.

30 April 1960

6 It is nice to think we can all still enjoy seeing this engine on the Torbay Steam Railway today, but here it was very much in everyday use and coupled up to "Dukedog" No. 9014 in the yard outside Croes Newydd shed.

Allocated to Oswestry shed No. 7827 **Lydham Manor** has just taken on water for the first leg of the journey to Pwllheli.

30 April 1960

7 In this picture the pair are moving off shed on their way to Ruabon to take over a special train of members of the Festiniog Railway Preservation Society.

30 April 1960

8 No. 1021 **County of Montgomery** crosses a new set of points with flat bottom track at Llangollen line junction just to the south of Ruabon. It will have worked all the way from London, to return in the early hours of Sunday morning with two sleeping cars added to the formation. This photograph clearly shows the highest part of a Great Western engine.

30 April 1960

9 After the engine change at Ruabon the "Manor" and "Dukedog" are seen at the west end of Corwen goods yard with the road bridge in the background carrying the A5 on its way to Holyhead.
30 April 1960

10 I believe Inspector Jack Hancock is silhouetted standing on the far side of the footplate just after the train has passed Llanuwchllyn station. Arrival at Minffordd was some 15 minutes before the advertised time.
30 April 1960

11 On our overcrowded roads today chasing trains is hazardous but with little traffic about in April of that year my Morris Minor was clearly the faster of the two means of transport. I am sure the bird is a seagull but why black I do not know. Anyway it adds to the nautical atmosphere as the train comes off the bridge and into Barmouth.
30 April 1960

12 The final picture for the day was taken at Pwllheli shed and shows the "Dukedog" serviced and waiting for the night to fall before setting out again to cross the Welsh mountains.

30 April 1960

13 Taken from the passenger footbridge at Southam Road and Harbury Station an afternoon local train from Banbury to Leamington is just leaving, with the porter about to take the tickets from the passengers in the foreground.

6 May 1960

14 Southam Road and Harbury Station was over a mile from Harbury village and even farther to Southam. In this view taken in 1974 a "Western" class diesel Hydraulic passes the site of the former station and goods yard.

It is interesting to compare the two pictures on this page as only the hut for the P.W. gang remains and at the time of writing this class of diesel will not be with us much longer.

16 July 1974

15 Another picture at Southam Road and Harbury Station with No. 6004 **King George III** ascending the gradient with the up "Cambrian Coast Express".

6 May 1960

16 With the arrival of the diesel a number of "King" class engines were allocated to Cardiff Canton shed to work the South Wales expresses to London. No. 6009 **King Charles II** passes Little Somerford station at high speed with the driver and fireman looking out of the cab. The 702 reporting numbers covered the 08.30 Cardiff to Paddington.

14 May 1960

17 A delightful scene not expected on the main line, but standing in the down platform at Little Somerford on a glorious spring morning is a pick-up freight from Swindon with 0-4-2T No. 5815 in charge. The goods yard layout is of interest and also the double slip points on the down line above the guard's van.

14 May 1960

18 The object of visiting Little Somerford was to see an "Ian Allan" special pass through with No. 6000 **King George V** in charge.

The sun shone through the stormy sky as the train came up the 1 in 400 gradient at 83 m.p.h. and running nearly 15 minutes ahead of time. In fact, the train was so early that a number of enthusiasts missed it, having come many miles armed with cameras to see "his majesty" hard at work.

14 May 1960

20 The "Severn and Wessex Express" ran from Paddington to Severn Tunnel Junction and back to Bath for a journey over the Somerset and Dorset line.

Here, 2-6-0 No. 6384 runs into Bath past the shed where S. and D. 2-8-0 No. 53807 awaits to take the train to Bournemouth.

14 May 1960

19 No. 6912 **Helmster Hall** is working hard on the climb up to Wootton Bassett with an up fast freight train comprising mainly of coal from South Wales. There is plenty of detail visible in the signals for the railway modellers.

14 May 1960

21 On the way home from Bath I again halted at Wootton Bassett and saw two trains take the South Wales main line. No. 4094 **Dynevor Castle** has just come off the main line from Paddington to Bath and the signalman has certainly returned the signals to danger very quickly. Notice the old guard's van on the right of the picture leading a retired life away from all the activity.

14 May 1960

22 The signals are those as shown in picture No. 19 and it looks as if No. 6820 **Kingstone Grange** is fresh from overhaul at Swindon works before returning to its home shed at Worcester.

14 May 1960

23 I took the Sunday 12.25 from Chester home to Leamington Spa and it was
hauled as far as Wolverhampton by No. 6934 **Beachamwell Hall.**
    The scene is Shrewsbury station where the train stopped from 13.40 to 13.48.
Note the clock and also the fireman climbing up on the engine.

26 June 1960

24 Hardly necessary for a caption to this photograph so it must be platform 10 at
Paddington station and shows No. 6006 **King George I** after arrival with the
11.35 from Wolverhampton.
    The crew will be leaning out of the other side of the locomotive talking to any
passengers who can't resist the temptation to stop and admire the machinery at
the front of their train. The regulator handle looks well polished!

30 June 1960

25 At this period between 08.30 and 20.10 there were no less than 14 express departures each weekday from Paddington to Wolverhampton via Bicester. Twelve of these had restaurant cars, and buffet cars were included in the other two. Today there is one train a day via Bicester.

No. 6015 **King Richard III** stands in Platform 2 with the 15.10 to Wolverhampton and was allowed 100 minutes for the non-stop run to Leamington Spa which is 87¼ miles from Paddington.

30 June 1960

26 I took this photograph as it is unusual to be able to study the top of the boiler of a "King" at rest. Notice the safety valves, cladding fittings, whistles, and ventilators in the cab roof together with the longitudinal taper of the firebox.

30 June 1960

27 A Sunday visit to Old Oak Common produced an interesting set of photographs including this one of No. 6012 **King Edward VI** standing by the coaling plant. It had worked the "Cambrian Coast Express" to Shrewsbury and back the day before. The pile of ashes and soot emphasize the problems of running steam engines using coal as the energy source. Note the cycle tyre hanging against the wall.

3 July 1960

28   Out in the yard No. 6018 **King Henry VI** and No. 7017 **G.J. Churchward** await the next call of duty. The tender of the ''Castle'' is being replenished and if I remember correctly the ''King'' was on stand-by in case of any diesel failure.

3 July 1960

29 Standing inside the top passenger shed just by the door was No. 6000 **King George V** complete with bell and having been cleaned all over leaving the buffers and frames shining with oil in the dim light.

I like to see the massive construction showing the Whitworth nuts and bolts and the beautifully formed heads of the rivets.

3 July 1960

30 Here is a line-up of 0-6-0 tank engines used for shunting the carriage sidings and taking the empty stock to and from Paddington.

No. 1507 was one of the ten outside cylinder short wheelbase engines built in 1949 and spent part of its life in South Wales before moving to London. Careful study of this picture will emphasize the ease of maintenance and ability to reach all moving parts. Notice the padlock on the toolbox adjacent to the cab steps.

3 July 1960

31 At Old Oak Common the engines were cleaned inside the shed, and with its large allocation of express engines arranged around the four turntables, the atmosphere of living with steam engines was exhilarating.

This, the largest depot of the Great Western Railway, was built in 1906 and the view shows No. 6973 **Bricklehampton Hall** and No. 4096 **Highclere Castle** facing south-east with the south turntable in the foreground.

3 July 1960

33 Headboards galore are leaning against the shed office from where they are collected by the crew for fitting on the smoke-box lamp iron before leaving the depot. On the left are two samples of "The Merchant Venturer" 11.05 Paddington to Weston-super-Mare followed by the "Torbay Express" 12.00 Paddington-Kingswear and against the wall is the "South Wales Pullman" 08.50 Paddington to Swansea. The right side is not so easy with their riveted repairs. The "Inter-City" 09.00 Paddington to Wolverhampton followed by an un-identifiable headboard probably "The Cambrian Coast Express". Leaning against the wall is the multi-coloured version of the "Inter-City".

32 Superheater elements are leaning against the buffer beam of a member of the "4700" class followed by L.M.S. 2-8-0 No. 48431, No. 7903 Foremarke Hall and No. 6023 King Edward II.

The engines are stabled off the north turntable and looking due east, so readers can easily identify the location.

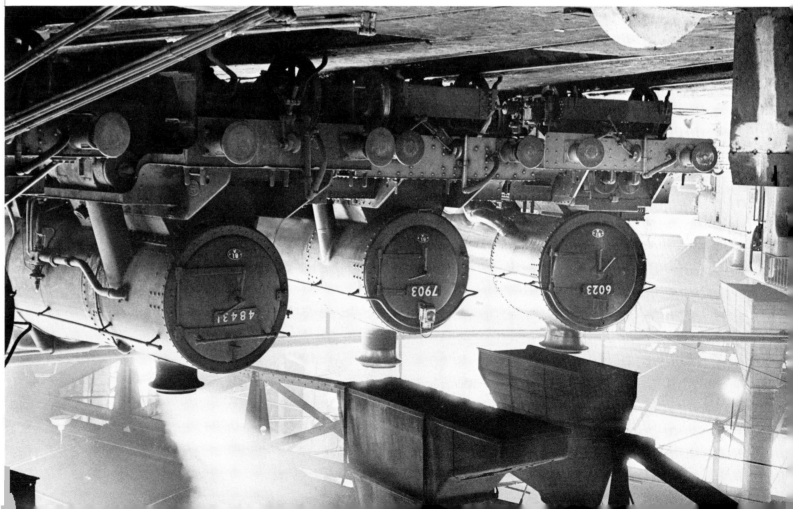

34   The final picture at Old Oak Common shows the south turntable and of particular interest is the 65 ft. under girder turntable which is completely boarded over to allow the staff easy access. The design of the roof is also of interest, bearing in mind that the size of the building is 360 ft. x 444 ft.

From left to right can be seen No. 5981 **Frensham Hall**, No. 6973 **Bricklehampton Hall** and No. 7032 **Denbigh Castle**.

3 July 1960

35   No. 6000 **King George V**, seen here working the down "Cambrian Coast Express", on one of the fastest stretches of track covered during its journey. Fosse Box signal box is behind the engine and with the speed into the 80s the exposure was 1/1000 of a second at f4.

8 July 1960

36 I hope this picture will give encouragement to those involved in restoring this fine engine at Quainton Road near Aylesbury. It is certainly in good condition here as it takes the up "Inter-City" on the embankment from Whitnash to Harbury.

15 July 1960

37 The Autumn special train to Swindon of the "Stephenson Locomotive Society" leaves Leamington Spa wrong line working on a Sunday morning. This was the last time I saw No. 3440 **City of Truro** in steam before it was withdrawn in May the following year for preservation in the Swindon Railway Museum.

4 September 1960

38 A view of Warwick goods yard looking north with 2-6-2T No. 5101 assisting an iron ore train at the beginning of Hatton Bank. The yard is now an oil storage complex, with all rail facilities and signals removed and a fence erected beside the down line.

As usual the train engine is one of the stalwarts of the G.W.R., namely a 2-8-0 No. 2874.

10 September 1960

39 At Swindon shed stabled roung the east turntable stand No. 6993 **Arthog Hall** and ex-works No. 5095 **Barbury Castle.**

11 September 1960

40 You may remember the long walk at Swindon Works along the side of the main line down to "A" shop. The first sight of an ex-works engine took place by a turntable out in the open. With a collection of ashpans on the right 2-8-0 No. 4701 and "Britannia" Pacific No. 70022 **Tornado** have been undergoing steam tests.

11 September 1960

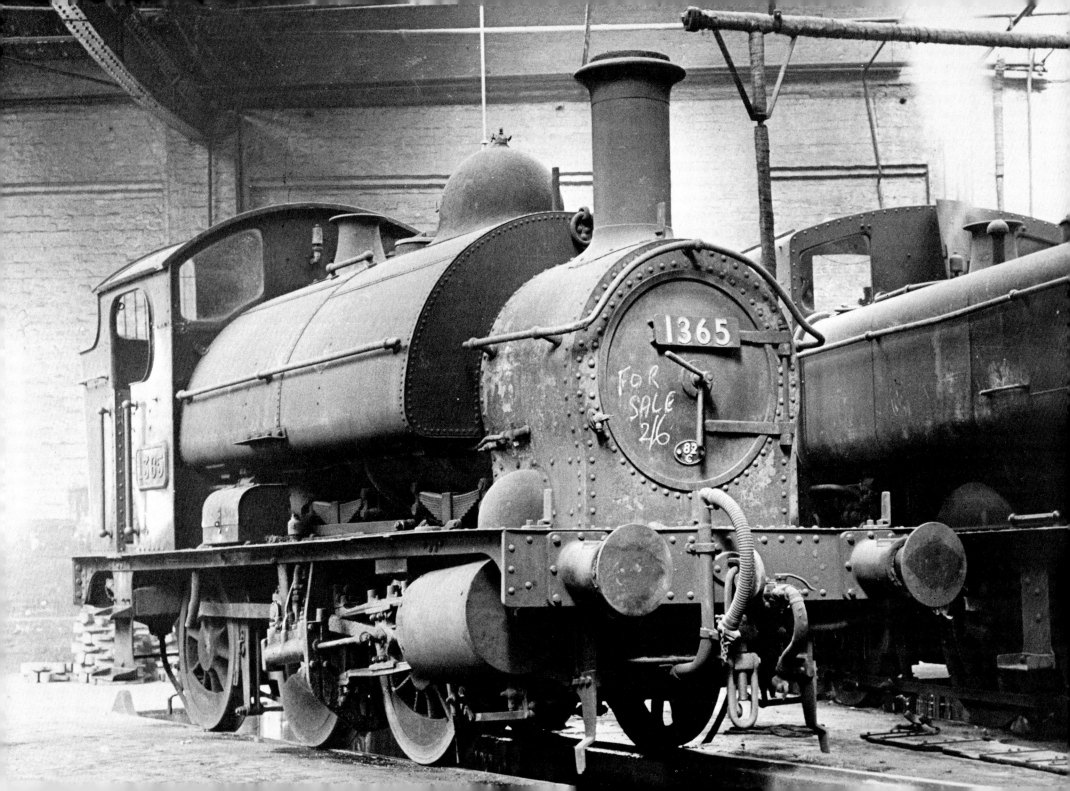

41 Built in 1910 for use in dock areas where there are sharp curves 0-6-0 saddle tank No. 1365 ended its days at Swindon and is shown here next to the west turntable. Even though it appears to be "marked up" at a very low price this did not prevent it from being cut up after withdrawal in November 1962.

11 September 1960

42 Now beautifully preserved at Swindon Railway Museum, "Dean Goods" 0-6-0 No. 2516 awaits restoration as it stands outside Swindon works. Built in 1897 it survived two world wars and was withdrawn from Oswestry shed in May 1956.

11 September 1960

43 A contrast of beauty and functional design is apparent in this view outside "A" shop at Swindon works.

Originally built at Crewe 2-10-0 No. 92006 has just emerged from a major overhaul and together with No. 6019 **King Henry V** they are awaiting to be united with their tenders before steam tests and running in.

11 September 1960

44   This detail is a view of the rocking levers used to drive the outside piston valves on No. 6019 **King Henry V.**

Accessibility to the motion on four-cylinder Great Western engines was always a problem and this picture gives an idea of what it was all about.

11 September 1960

45   No. 4086 **Builth Castle** is under repair at Swindon works flanked by a "Mogul" and "Hall" class locomotive.

11 September 1960

46 This picture is full of interest and I wonder if "Wally" still works at Swindon!
Apart from No. 6008 **King James II** nearing the end of a major overhaul there is the frame and cab side of No. 7026 **Tenby Castle** and also one of the early "Warship" diesels. In the right foreground are stacked vacuum brake cylinders with piston rod protruding at the top.

11 September 1960

47 A study in chimney shapes outside Swindon shed with No. 4969 **Shrugborough Hall**, No. 1010 **County of Caernarvon**, Class B1 No. 61137 and 7022 **Hereford Castle**.

11 September 1960

48 No. 7811 **Dunley Manor** heads out of Shrewsbury and past the shed with a train for Aberystwyth. This lovely autumn day started with a thick mist and it was just beginning to clear when the picture was taken.

24 September 1960

49 As the mist lifts 2-6-0 No. 7330 moves out of Shrewsbury shed to take on water before working the "Talyllyn Railway Preservation Society Special" to Towyn.

24 September 1960

50 Just about to couple on to the "Mogul" is "Dukedog" No. 9017 now preserved on the Bluebell line. This engine, the last of the "Dukedogs" to run, was withdrawn the following month. They will always be remembered for the coupling rods which used to flash up and down in the sunlight when travelling at speed.

24 September 1960

51 Hauling the "Talyllyn Railway Preservation Society Special" from Paddington to Shrewsbury was 2-8-0 No. 4701 resplendent in lined-out green livery. It is shown here with steam shut off and coasting down into Shrewsbury.

Note the snifting valves on the outside of the steam chest which was standard on only four members of the class.

24 September 1960

52 As a farewell to the "Dukedogs" I must include this my last photograph of them, climbing away from Shrewsbury in the brilliant sunshine with a rake of B.R. stock.

24 September 1960

53 Soon after the "Talyllyn Railway Preservation Society Special" had departed I waited for the up "Cambrian Coast Express" which appeared behind No. 7818 **Granville Manor** and 0-6-0 No. 2200. The train continued to London behind No. 5059 **Earl St. Aldwyn** and after a mad dash to Upton Magna in the car I caught the train coming through in fine style on its way to Wolverhampton.

24 September 1960

54 The down "Cambrian Coast Express" arrived in Shrewsbury behind No. 6015 **King Richard III** and after an engine change it is seen here on its way to Aberystwyth behind No. 7818 **Granville Manor.**

On a Saturday the rake of B.R. stock always had an ex-L.N.E.R. coach leading and I have never yet had an explanation for this unusual working.

24 September 1960

55 The breakdown crane is just visible on the right of the picture as 0-6-0PT No. 8781 shunts across the South Wales main line outside Shrewsbury shed.

24 September 1960

56 In the distance a passenger train disappears towards Chester and a "Hall" class engine is just visible under the road bridge. Meanwhile, on the right No. 1025 **County of Radnor** crosses the line leading out of Shrewsbury station for Crewe and the north-west.

An interesting example of trackwork is the reason for including this picture.

24 September 1960

57 Back at Shrewsbury shed, I went in search of No. 6015 **King Richard III** which would shortly be returning to London with an afternoon express. After servicing and coaled up ready for the road the engine is seen leaving for Shrewsbury station.
24 September 1960

58 No. 7025 **Sudeley Castle** is having the ash removed from its smokebox after working the 08.00 Plymouth-Liverpool train. This engine, of course, comes off at Shrewsbury to be replaced by a London Midland engine for the journey onto Liverpool.

24 September 1960

59 A general view of Shrewsbury shed showing the Great Western Railway section on the left and the London Midland on the right. No. 4701 is awaiting to take the "Talyllyn Railway Preservation Society Special" back to London in the early hours of the next morning and No. 7821 **Ditcheat Manor** on a train from the Welsh coast is held at the signals, while a Class 5 can be seen taking on water.

24 September 1960

60 Many of the "Manor" class engines were kept very clean but this one, No. 7815 **Fritwell Manor,** is an exception as it leaves Shrewsbury for Aberystwyth at 15.57 according to the clock on the Abbey. Note the complement of G.W.R. coaches.

24 September 1960

62 Newbury Races was always a great day for steam specials and the first on this Saturday morning was hauled by No. 7037 **Swindon.** Up above, as luck would have it, was a De Havilland Chipmunk coming in to land at White Waltham airfield.

4 March 1961

61 Just two days after Christmas and the last picture of the year. I have included my favourite piece of machinery No. 6000 **King George V** climbing Hatton Bank with the 09.10 Paddington-Birkenhead train. Do not be confused by the wheels being below rail level as the goods loop is unfortunately at a slightly higher level.

27 December 1960

63   The members' train going to Newbury Races was made up of first-class stock and always had an immaculate locomotive, usually a "King" class. In this case it is a double-chimney "Castle" No. 5056 **Earl of Powis** passing White Waltham complete with Great Western restaurant car.

4 March 1961

64 Wellington boots are very much the part of a railway photographer's equipment, although on this sunny spring day they were not required. D821 **Greyhound** flashes past on an up Weston-super-Mare express with the passenger in the third compartment fast asleep — probably because he was the only one with his window closed!

4 March 1961

65 The same location beside White Waltham airfield. No. 6019 **King Henry V** has 13 bogies in tow as it nears the end of its journey from Cardiff to Paddington with "The Red Dragon". This is another example of the small allocation of "King" class engines to Cardiff Canton for working the London trains.

4 March 1961

66 I should have liked to acquire a photograph of this engine on the traverser outside "A" shop at Swindon works after it had received its major overhaul. However, the next best was to see it in service as shown in picture No. 88. No. 5078 **Beaufort** is just visible with "Warship" diesels inside the works.

30 March 1961

67 No. 4073 **Caerphilly Castle** was withdrawn from service in May 1960. It stood outside the stock shed until work commenced on the restoration necessary for its presentation to the Science Museum in London.

This photograph clearly shows the enormous amount of work which was undertaken, the engine being completely stripped and sent out as new. The preservationists working at steam centres in this country today would envy the facilities available here.

30 March 1961

68 Through carriages and restaurant car from Newcastle to Bournemouth West headed by No. 7911 **Lady Margaret Hall** hurry through Beaulieu Road station in the New Forest.

This engine was shedded at Oxford and named after the ladies' college at the University. When my twin sister was up at Oxford, indeed at Lady Margaret Hall, she used to come home to Leamington behind this engine which always gave me a kick but probably the female sex was not impressed!

24 June 1961

69 Most pictures taken during the afternoon in Harbury Cutting are from the sunny side. However, the shadow side is sometimes attractive and would have been more so had the engine been clean. No. 6022 **King Edward III** had worked up to London on the 09.35 Wolverhampton and is shown returning at speed on the 16.10 Paddington to Birkenhead.

22 July 1961

70 Shortly after Old Oak Common West Junction the Birmingham line passes under a bridge carrying a freight line from Acton to Willesden and the Midland at Cricklewood. No. 5090 **Neath Abbey** passes beneath this bridge with the 15.10 Paddington-Wolverhampton train which was always worked by an engine from 81A.
26 July 1961

71 Turning further round from the previous picture No. 6022 **King Edward III** is seen accelerating the 16.10 Paddington-Birkenhead away from Old Oak Common.

The line in the foreground, long since removed, used to carry trains from the Great Western Railway down through Olympia and to the Southern Railway.
26 July 1961

THE WESTMINSTER ENGINEERING CO LTD

72 When I took this picture I did not realise that No. 4086 **Builth Castle** would be withdrawn early the following year but I did assume the writing was on the wall for all the class. In this scene a through working of Southern stock passes Leamington Spa South Junction signal box on its way north with returning holidaymakers. The significance of the broken cars is quite obvious.

5 August 1961

73 In human terms these two must have been exchanging pleasantries. Indeed, it makes one wonder if the driver of No. 6025 **King Henry III** intentionally pulled up early so that they could converse! The 09.10 Paddington-Birkenhead train is at Leamington Spa General with a d.m.u. waiting in the bay to proceed to Stratford-upon-Avon.

7 August 1961

74 "Hall" class engines were very unusual on the up "Cambrian Coast Express" as it was very much the domain of the "Kings". Deputizing for a failure No. 4947 **Nanhoran Hall** from Bristol Bath Road shed climbs past Fosse Box and making some good black smoke from what looks like a load of indifferent coal in the tender.

7 August 1961

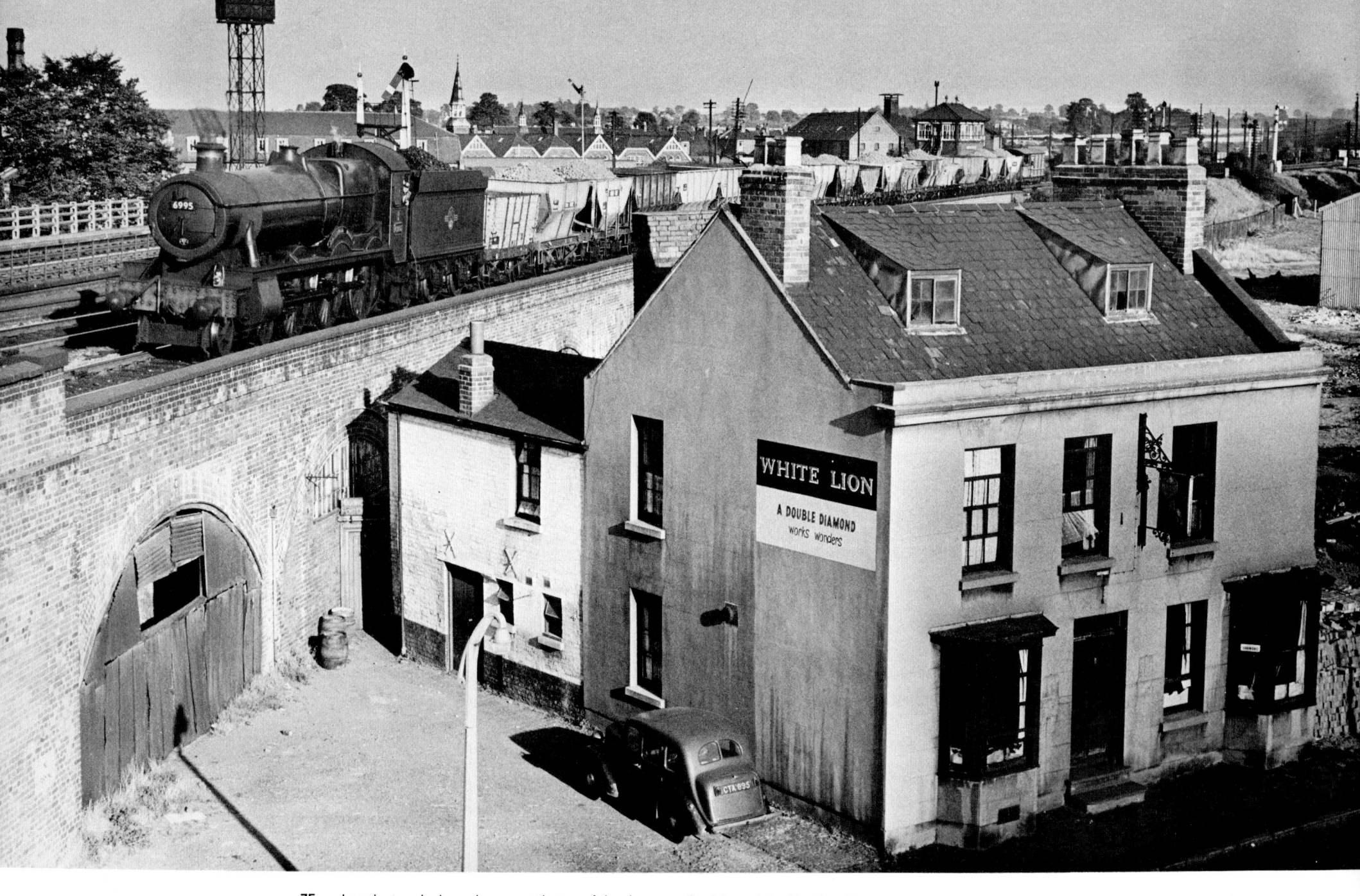

75 Leamington shed may be seen at the top of the picture on the right and the Warnford Hospital stands out behind No. 6995
Benthall Hall as it approaches the station over a brick viaduct with an iron ore train from Banbury.
The White Lion has since been demolished and the site is now an industrial complex.

29 August 1961

I spent a day around Saunderton and drove from Leamington in thick fog hoping that the sun would appear when I reached Princes Risborough.

Just minutes before the 09.10 Paddington-Birkenhead ran through the station the light appeared and No. 6024 **King Edward I** looked a magnificent sight as it swept by with a 12-wheel sleeping car leading the train. The d.m.u. in the bay platform will be for Oxford via Thame.

2 September 1961

GT WESTERN & GT CENTRAL JOINT COMMITTEE
NOTICE
THIS FOOTPATH
IS FOR THE USE OF PEDESTRIANS ONLY

THE GT WESTERN & GT CENTRAL JOINT COMMITTEE
HEREBY GIVE NOTICE THAT SECTION 17 OF THE GT WESTERN &
GT CENTRAL JOINT COMMITTEE ACT 1933 PROVIDES AS FOLLOWS
ANY PERSON WHO SHALL RIDE A BICYCLE
TRICYCLE MOTOR-CYCLE OR OTHER SIMILAR MACHINE
OR BRING ANY HANDCART OR BARROW OR SIMILAR
CONVEYANCE UPON ANY FOOTBRIDGE FOOTPATH
OR CAUSEWAY OR THROUGH ANY SUBWAY BELONGING
TO THE COMMITTEE AND MADE OR SET APART FOR THE
USE OR ACCOMMODATION OF PEDESTRIANS ONLY
SHALL ON SUMMARY CONVICTION BE LIABLE TO A
PENALTY NOT EXCEEDING FORTY SHILLINGS

77 Maybe this notice is still by the line above Princes Risborough station but it is a typical example of how to confuse simple sort of people like me. Although I do enjoy the wording the punch line is at the end and you may have to read it again to see if the moped you are riding qualifies!

2 September 1961

78 On the up line between Princes Risborough and Saunderton there is a short tunnel which No. 6007 **King William III** has just left and is seen here continuing the climb at 1 in 167 to the summit of the Chiltern Hills.

The train is the 11.35 Wolverhampton-Paddington with a Hawkesworth coach, probably built just after Nationalization.

2 September 1961

79 A Sunday morning back at Old Oak Common shed with Driver George Green and his fireman Douglas Godden standing in front of No. 6000 **King George V** which they were taking out to Birmingham with a Sunday excursion.

24 September 1961

80 Out in the yard and No. 6000 **King George V** is slowly moving backwards on its way to Paddington station to pick up its train. Note the siding signal allowing the engine out of the yard.

24 September 1961

81 No. 5041 **Tiverton Castle** was shedded at Neath (87A) in South Wales and is being serviced at Old Oak Common prior to returning home. No. 1500 requires no comment. The picture says all that is necessary when comparing the two engines.

24 September 1961

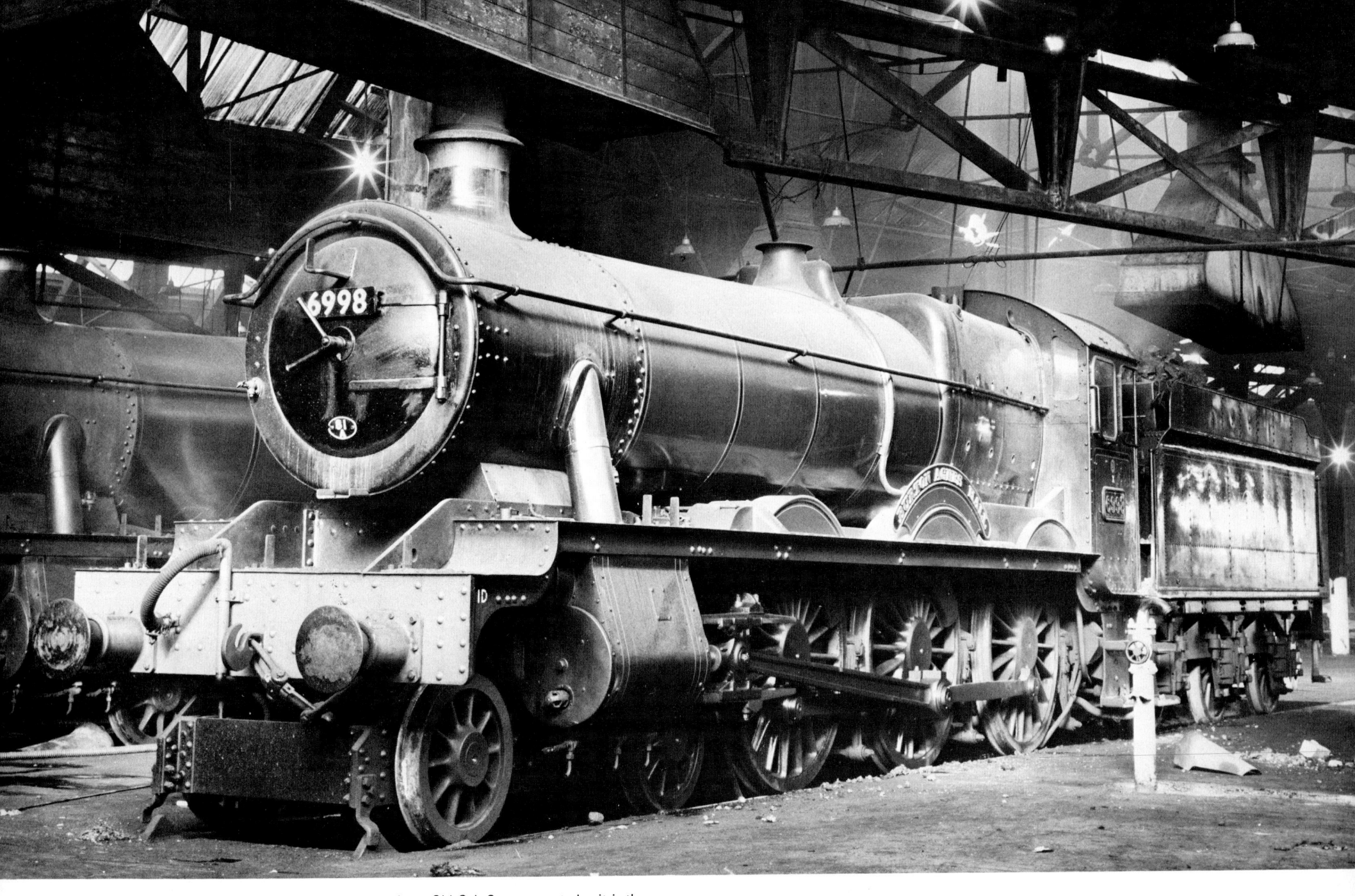

82 How lucky to find this engine ex-works at Old Oak Common as today it is the only "Hall" class locomotive passed for main-line running. No. 6998 **Burton Agnes Hall** stands off the south-west turntable with a light covering of dust on the boiler barrel.

The letters ID painted on the footplate angle iron immediately behind the buffer beam signify that the engine has "improved draughting".

24 September 1961

83 No. 6012 **King Edward VI** sparkles in a ray of sunshine where it has been stabled next to three B.R. Class 9 2-10-0 freight engines.

24 September 1961

84 You will notice the way in which all the oil and grease has been burnt off the axle-box and axle due to the bearing running hot.

The wheel is the front nearside on the bogie of a "Castle" class locomotive and the picture taken in the repair shop gives an indication as to how dirt collects on the more inaccessible parts. Note the lubrication pipe protruding with its cork stopper.

24 September 1961

85 In the background loaded coal wagons are shunted up to the coal stage. On the left of the picture and in the foreground the tender of No. 7009 **Athelney Castle** has just been filled with water. The chain flies through the air as the pipe is swung clear of the tender.

24 September 1961

86　Monday afternoon at Paddington with steam deputizing for a failure of the "Blue Pullman". With a 16.50 departure No. 7033 **Hartlebury Castle** will have some fast running to reach Leamington, the first stop in 89 minutes.

　　The set of Pullman stock was kept at Old Oak Common in case one of the Diesel Pullman units should not be available for service.

25 September 1961

87　No. 7006 **Lydford Castle** has just backed onto its train and the fireman is jumping down to collect his lamp from the platform. With the clock in the background saying 17.00 there is plenty of time to get the engine prepared for the 17.15 departure to Worcester and Hereford.

25 September 1961

88 Platform No. 10 at Paddington where No. 7011 **Banbury Castle** has not quite reached the end of the line but awaits its turn to move light engine back to Ranelagh Yard for servicing before returning to Worcester in the afternoon.

The engine had worked up with the "Cathedrals Express" — the only titled train on the Worcester line.

26 September 1961

89 Do you ever thank the driver at the end of a safe journey? It certainly looks as if this driver has not been complimented on his performance judging by the look on his face, after the last passenger to leave the 09.35 Wolverhampton-Paddington train turned to look at the engine as he left Platform No. 7.

The two photographs show the single and double chimney "Castles" and also which side of the station is best illuminated for photography.

26 September 1961

90   I must have been on holiday during the week this picture was taken. The time would be around 11.40 and No. 6029 **King Edward VIII** is passing Warwick station with the down 10.10 ''Birmingham Pullman''. Although the diesel electric ''Blue Pullman'' was fairly reliable, steam seemed a too regular substitute in the early days.

27 September 1961

91   2-8-0 No. 4704 runs into Shrewsbury with the ''Talyllyn Railway Preservation Society Special'' train from Paddington to Towyn. The elegant cast-iron chimney is clearly shown as well as an exemplary state of cleanliness.

Although specialist sources of information state that this engine had sniffing valves on the outside of the steam chests, at this stage in its life they must have been above the platform in the usual position.

30 September 1961

92 The "Talyllyn Railway Preservation Society Special" was on the single line from Shrewsbury and this caused the up "Cambrian Coast Express" headed by No. 7803 **Barcote Manor** to be stopped at Buttington Junction. The fireman has been down to the signal box obviously annoyed that in getting the fire in good shape for the climb ahead it is producing unwanted steam.

The siding went to a brick works across the main road and can you see the smoke from a set of thrashing tackle on the right of the picture?

30 September 1961

93 How fortunate that this section of the Cambrian line has been saved, running as it does along the north shore of the River Dovey.

2-6-2T No. 5555 and Collett 0-6-0 No. 2222 are nearing the end of their journey from Shrewsbury to Towyn and passing Panteidal near Aberdovey.

30 September 1961

94   For a short time the up "Inter-City" was double-headed by a "Castle" and "King" or two "Castle" class locomotives.
       The sun is getting low in the sky at this time of the year and produces a dramatic lighting effect as No. 5089 **Westminster Abbey** and No. 6021 **King Richard II** leave Leamington Spa. The signal post, above the second coach, denuded of its arm, used to allow trains at the South Junction crossing to join the line from Leamington to Rugby.

6 October 1961

No. 6021 **King Richard II** starts away from Leamington Spa with the 14.35 Wolverhampton-Paddington train. The station is just out of the picture on the left and you will notice the enormous brick viaduct which is used by both the L.M.S. and G.W.R. lines.

One of the six largest parish churches in England, All Saints dominates the skyline at the south end of the town.

28 October 1961

96   Another view at Leamington Spa General station with No. 6008 **King James II** standing at the up platform with the 10.35 Wolverhampton-Paddington train.

The driver has been round the engine with an oil-can topping up the lubricators and Bert Smith starts down the train to tap the carriage wheels and check that all is in order.

28 October 1961

97   This is one of my really lucky pictures with a flash of winter sunshine coming through a very dark sky just at the right moment.

     2-8-0 No. 48751 has backed into the up goods siding at Southam Road and Harbury station to enable No. 6005 **King George II** to pass by with the 11.35 Wolverhampton-Paddington train.

2 December 1961

98 Another dull day without any sign of sunshine but fortunately the front engine is making a worth-while smoke effect.

No. 6911 **Holker Hall** and No. 4082 **Windsor Castle** approach Hatton station with an overloaded 09.10 Paddington-Birkenhead train.

17 February 1962

99 Leaving Leamington Spa and into a hazy sunshine No. 6023 **King Edward II** accelerates the train shown in the adjoining photograph.

14 March 1962

100 This picture marked the beginning of the end for the "King" class so far as I was concerned. A dirty engine recently stabled at Stafford Road with a Cardiff Canton shed plate still in position. My favourite, No. 6006 **King George I,** had already been withdrawn in the preceding month and the complete class had disappeared before the end of the year.

In the first part of the morning at this time there were fast trains to London via Bicester leaving Leamington at 08.00, 08.08, 08.30 and 09.25. This picture shows the arrival of the 07.35 Wolverhampton-Paddington train at Leamington Spa, headed by No. 6023 **King Edward II.**

14 March 1962

101 I believe this engine, No. 6011 **King James I,** was the last of the Stafford Road "King" class to receive a major overhaul earlier in the year. In this picture it is climbing away from Leamington Spa on a 1 in 240 gradient. The train is the 08.33 Wolverhampton-Paddington which ran non-stop to London, but just compare the load with that carried today by the Brush Type 4 diesel-electrics.

17 March 1962

102
103
Both these pictures were taken from Warwick goods yard and show the main line to Birmingham disappearing under the bridge in the background.

0-6-0PT No. 3619 (right) from Leamington shed has been put into the up Warwick goods loop to allow an express to pass. The signal is "off" for the 09.10 Paddington with No. 6021 **King Richard II** in charge.

In the lower photograph 0-6-0T No. 6604 in green livery shunts the yard — in this case petrol tank wagons for the storage terminal in the background.

Whilst not possessing the glamour of the express engines, the smaller engines shunting goods wagons to and fro was always a relaxing sight and if the approach was right a ride was often possible.

17 March 1962

104 Oxford shed has provided No. 5025 Chirk **Castle** as motive power for the 08.35 Bournemouth West to Wolverhampton complete with restaurant buffet and reserved seats if required at 2s 0d each. The engine is picking up water on Lapworth troughs and why is the handrail bent on the boiler side? See also picture 34. **17 March 1962**

105 Where the location is suitable I often preferred the broadside picture and this one is particularly interesting as the crew are leaning out of the window, the fireman probably having been firing most of the way up to Harbury Cutting from Leamington. No. 6020 **King Henry IV** has the 11.35 Wolverhampton-Paddington train with a Hawksworth coach leading. **24 April 1962**

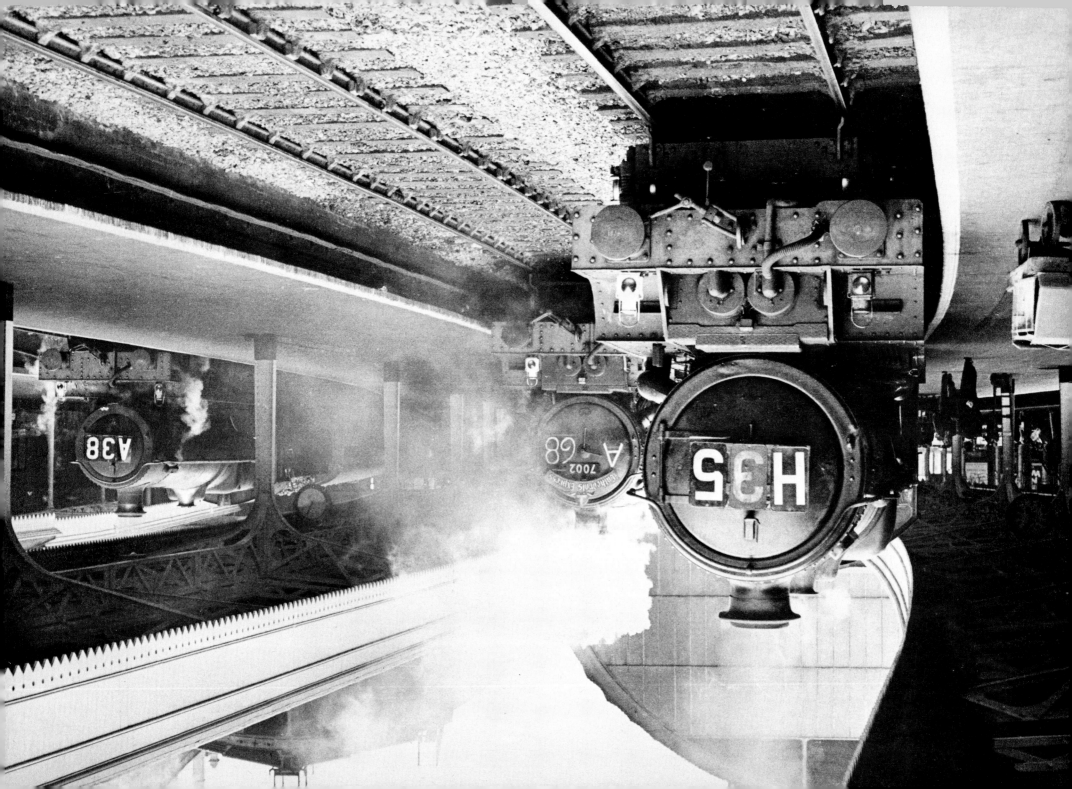

106

Here, No. 6027 **King Richard I** has the 17.10 down train to Wolverhampton and No. 7002 **Devizes Castle** the 17.15 "Cathedrals Express" to Worcester with through carriages to Hereford and Kidderminster. In Platform 2 an unidentified "Hall" class awaits departure with Platform 1 having just been vacated by No. 7034 **Ince Castle** with the "Cheltenham Spa Express". A scene full of activity and interest.

18 July 1962

107

Since I was travelling on the train hauled by No. 6027 **King Richard I** a compartment near the engine was always chosen and this picture was taken through the top sliding window. The driver is attending to the motion, and the reversing handwheel and speedometer are clearly shown.

In the background a "Hall" class engine moves into a platform underneath Bishops Bridge Road.

18 July 1962

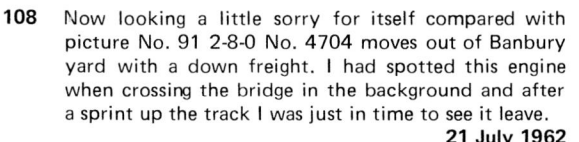

108 Now looking a little sorry for itself compared with picture No. 91 2-8-0 No. 4704 moves out of Banbury yard with a down freight. I had spotted this engine when crossing the bridge in the background and after a sprint up the track I was just in time to see it leave.

21 July 1962

109 At the north end of Banbury station No. 4961 **Pyrland Hall** awaits in the down bay while Class B1 No. 61028 **Umseke** is ready to leave for Woodford Halse with the 09.35 from Banbury.

Part of the new station is visible but today it is impossible to imagine the size of the railway operation which once was carried out non-stop throughout the 24 hours in the marshalling yards and locomotive depot.

21 July 1962

110 This can only be Reading station looking west with No. 5032 **Usk Castle** preparing to leave with the 09.15 Paddington to Hereford. I had travelled down from London to stay at Reading awhile to see the Newbury Race specials pass through behind No. 6000 and No. 6002. This was a sad occasion as they were all polished to perfection and it was the last time I ever saw a "King" class engine in service except for the odd special working.

14 September 1962

111

Walking up the central island platform at Reading gave one a sense of anticipation to see what was acting as the east end station pilot. Ready with express headlamps fitted, in case of a diesel failure, is No. 5979 **Cruckton Hall.**

At the west end of the station on similar duties could be found on the same day in spotless condition No. 5018 **St. Mawes Castle.**
14 September 1962

112

Since it was such a fine autumn day I decided to travel home to Leamington by diesel multiple unit and sat in the front seat behind the driver's compartment.

We were just pulling away from Radley when an up Worcester express came through the station behind No. 4089 **Donnington Castle.** Needless to say I had been waiting for it with Leica at the ready — a situation where the small 35 mm camera is always the best instrument.
14 September 1962

113 The final week-end in September was devoted to a pilgrimage to see No. 6000 **King George V** arrive at Ruabon with the Talyllyn Railway Special train from London.

  While waiting for the special train I saw No. 6928 **Underley Hall** come through the station with an up freight watched by engine spotters of the period.

29 September 1962

114 After developing a roll of film I always inspect each negative with an 8x magnifier to check for sharpness and blemishes. It was only after printing this picture that I realized the sinister shape above the safety valve bonnet of No. 1013 **County of Dorset** was a double-arm siding signal and not an imperfection on the negative.

  The freight train is accelerating down the gradient and away from Ruabon station.

29 September 1962

115 Turning round from the previous picture is the sight for which I had been waiting — the impeccably turned out engine just as it is today in preservation at H.P. Bulmers, Hereford. It must have taken many hours of preparation to look like this but the sight gave so much pleasure to admirers of the ''King'' class as most of them were inactive by this time.

Here, No. 6000 **King George V** has just shut off steam for the end of its journey at Ruabon.

29 September 1962

116 Under a threatening sky No. 7814 **Fringford Manor** brings a down train through the outskirts of Shrewsbury.

The first coach has the middle compartment removed allowing an automatic self-service buffet to be installed open to the corridor. This auto buffet dispensing snacks, soft drinks, confectionary and cigarettes was being tested instead of a restaurant buffet on the ''Cambrian Coast Express'' between Aberystwyth and Shrewsbury.

29 September 1962

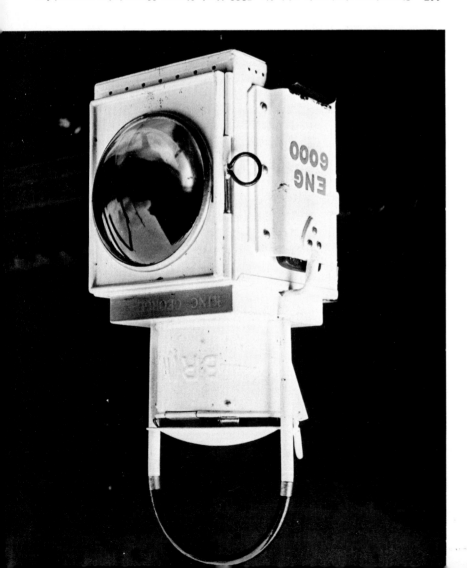

117 Shrewsbury shed again with No. 7823 **Hook Norton Manor** being prepared for work and standing by the coal stage. In the afternoon No. 6000 **King George V** had run light engine to Shrewsbury shed for servicing and I had already taken

118 many pictures when I came upon the tail lamp mounted on the tender. This detail shows the affection bestowed on this engine with the white-painted lamp body and engine number on the side. Of more interest is the brass plate above the lamp glass which is simply engraved "King George V".
29 September 1962

119 Study this picture. The "Warship" diesel hydraulic conveying through carriages from Glasgow and Liverpool to Plymouth is totally unloved. No one looks at it and indeed all the class have now been withdrawn. The schoolboy admiration for the steam engine survives and the scene could almost be a "Return to Steam" run of 1975. This picture shows No. 6000 **King George V** about to leave Shrewsbury station on the 17.10 to Wolverhampton stopping at all stations.
29 September 1962

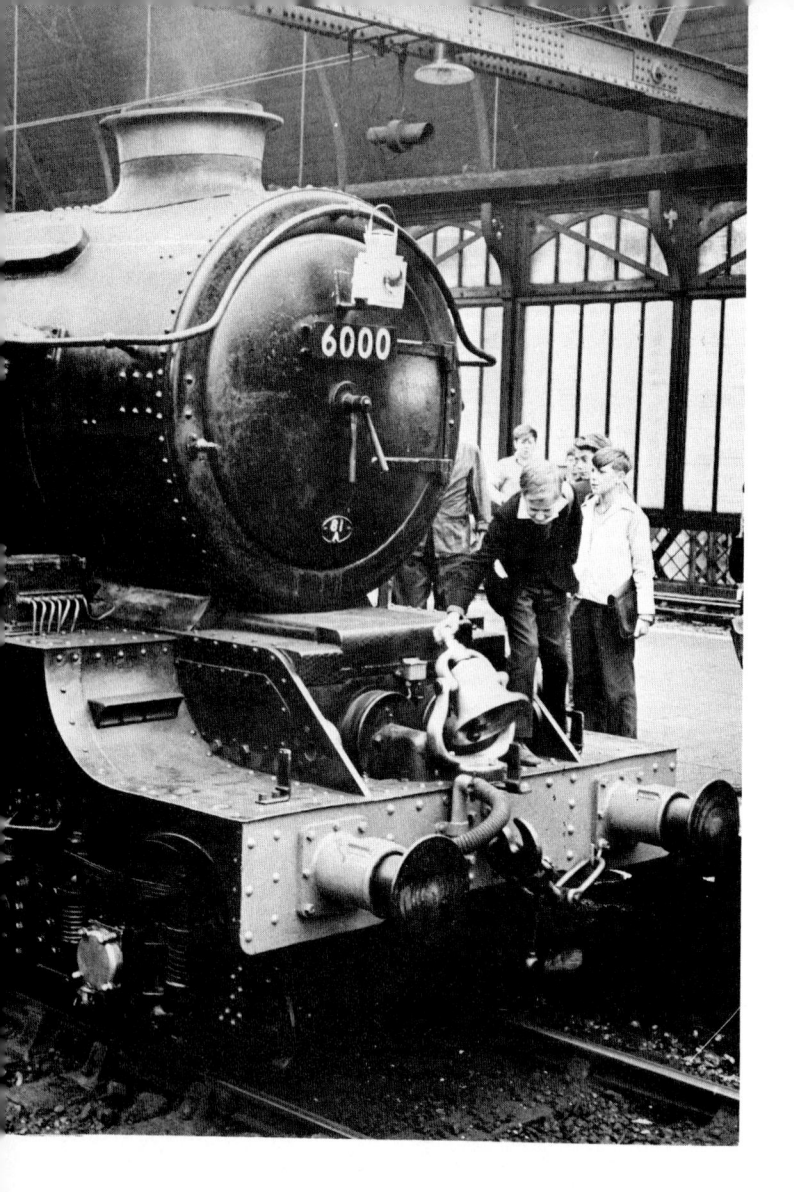

120
121 There seems little to say about these two pictures. The boy above takes his turn at ringing the bell and in the cab the rest of the throng queue up for the driver's autograph with one client obviously very satisfied.

29 September 1962